Georg Philipp
TELEMANN

(1681 – 1767)

Trio Sonata for 2 Treble (Alto) Recorders
and Basso continuo, TWV 42 : F 7
F Major / Fa majeur / F-Dur

Edited by
Manfredo Zimmermann

DOWANI International

Preface

This Trio Sonata in F Major for two treble (alto) recorders and basso continuo by Georg Philipp Telemann (TWV 42 : F 7) has been edited and recorded by Manfredo Zimmermann, professor of recorder at the Wuppertal Musikhochschule and a specialist in early music. This delightful and musicianly sonata places equal demands on the two recorder parts. Our volume is a revised edition with a new piano reduction.

The CD opens with the concert version of each movement. After tuning your instrument (Track 1), the musical work can begin. Our edition presents each solo part separately with harpsichord accompaniment at all three tempos, that is, one version allows you to play the first solo part and another the second. You thus have an opportunity to practice whichever part happens to be missing. However, there is no version that allows both solo parts to be played at once. At slow tempo, your own part can be heard softly in the background as a guide. The second and fourth movements are sensibly divided into subsections for practice purposes. You can select the subsection you want using the track numbers indicated in the solo part. Further explanations can be found at the end of this volume along with the names of the musicians involved in the recording. More detailed information can be found in the Internet at www.dowani.com. All of the versions were recorded live.

As befits its origins, this music relies heavily on elements of improvisation, and we have included only the most essential embellishments and phrase marks. Players are invited to add trills, mordents, slurs and so forth at their own discretion. The same holds true, of course, for the realization of the figured bass (basso continuo or harpsichord), as can clearly be heard on the recording.

We wish you lots of fun playing from our *DOWANI 3 Tempi Play Along* editions and hope that your musicality and diligence will enable you to play the concert version as soon as possible. Our goal is to provide the essential conditions you need for effective practicing through motivation, enjoyment and fun.

Your DOWANI Team

Avant-propos

Manfredo Zimmermann, professeur de flûte à bec au Conservatoire Supérieur de Wuppertal et spécialiste dans le domaine de la musique ancienne, a édité cette sonate en trio pour deux flûtes à bec alto et basse continue TWV 42 : F 7 en Fa majeur de Georg Philipp Telemann. La musique de cette sonate est enjouée bien que techniquement exigeante tant pour l'une que pour l'autre des deux parties de flûte à bec. La présente édition est une édition révisée avec une nouvelle réduction pour piano.

Le CD vous permettra d'entendre d'abord la version de concert de chaque mouvement. Après avoir accordé votre instrument (plage n° 1), vous pourrez commencer le travail musical. Dans cette édition, les deux parties de flûte à bec ont été enregistrées séparément dans les trois tempos avec accompagnement de clavecin. C'est-à-dire que vous trouverez une version avec laquelle vous pouvez jouer la première partie soliste et une autre version avec laquelle vous pouvez jouer la seconde partie soliste. Vous aurez donc la possibilité de travailler toujours la partie qui manque. Il n'existe, cependant, pas de version où vous pouvez jouer les deux parties solistes en même temps. Au tempo lent, la partie soliste choisie restera toujours audible très doucement à l'arrière-plan. Le deuxième et le quatrième mouvement ont été divisés en sections judicieuses pour faciliter le travail. Vous pouvez sélectionner ces sections à l'aide des numéros de plages indiqués dans la partie du soliste. Pour obtenir plus d'informations et les noms des artistes qui ont participé aux enregistrements, veuillez consulter la dernière page de cette édition ou notre site Internet : www.dowani.com. Toutes les versions ont été enregistrées en direct.

Cette musique repose à l'origine beaucoup sur des éléments d'improvisation ; c'est pourquoi nous n'avons ajouté que très peu d'ornements et de phrasés. Chaque musicien peut ou doit ajouter ses propres indications (trilles, mordants, liaisons etc.). Cela concerne également la réalisation de la basse chiffrée (basse continue ou clavecin) – comme on l'entend bien sur notre enregistrement.

Nous vous souhaitons beaucoup de plaisir à faire de la musique avec la collection *DOWANI 3 Tempi Play Along* et nous espérons que votre musicalité et votre application vous amèneront aussi rapidement que possible à la version de concert. Notre but est de vous offrir les bases nécessaires pour un travail efficace par la motivation et le plaisir.

Les Éditions DOWANI

Vorwort

Manfredo Zimmermann, Professor für Blockflöte an der Musikhochschule Wuppertal und Spezialist für Alte Musik, hat die vorliegende Triosonate für zwei Altblockflöten und Basso continuo TWV 42 : F 7 in F-Dur von Georg Philipp Telemann herausgegeben. Bei dieser außerordentlich musikantischen Triosonate sind beide Blockflötenstimmen gleichermaßen gefordert. Die vorliegende Ausgabe ist eine revidierte Neuausgabe mit einem neuen Klavierauszug.

Auf der CD können Sie zuerst die Konzertversion eines jeden Satzes anhören. Nach dem Stimmen Ihres Instrumentes (Track 1) kann die musikalische Arbeit beginnen. Bei dieser Ausgabe sind beide Solostimmen jeweils separat mit Cembalobegleitung in allen drei Tempi aufgenommen worden. Das bedeutet, dass es eine Version gibt, bei der die erste Solostimme mitgespielt werden kann und eine weitere, bei der die zweite Solostimme mitgespielt werden kann. Sie haben also die Möglichkeit, die jeweils fehlende Stimme zu üben. Es gibt allerdings keine Version, bei der beide Solostimmen gleichzeitig mitgespielt werden können. Im langsamen Tempo ist die eigene Stimme als Orientierung leise im Hintergrund zu hören. Der zweite und vierte Satz wurde in sinnvolle Übe-Abschnitte unterteilt. Diese können Sie mit Hilfe der in der jeweiligen Solostimme angegebenen Track-Nummern auswählen. Weitere Erklärungen hierzu sowie die Namen der Künstler finden Sie auf der letzten Seite dieser Ausgabe; ausführlichere Informationen können Sie im Internet unter www.dowani.com nachlesen. Alle eingespielten Versionen wurden live aufgenommen.

Da diese Musik ihrem Ursprung entsprechend sehr stark auf improvisatorischen Elementen beruht, wurden nur die nötigsten Verzierungen und Phrasierungen hinzugefügt. Der Spieler oder die Spielerin darf/soll gerne eigene Ergänzungen (Triller, Mordente, Bindungen etc.) vornehmen. Dies gilt natürlich auch für die Ausführung des Generalbasses (Basso continuo oder Cembalo) – wie in der Aufnahme deutlich zu hören ist.

Wir wünschen Ihnen viel Spaß beim Musizieren mit unseren *DOWANI 3 Tempi Play Along*-Ausgaben und hoffen, dass Ihre Musikalität und Ihr Fleiß Sie möglichst bald bis zur Konzertversion führen werden. Unser Ziel ist es, Ihnen durch Motivation, Freude und Spaß die notwendigen Voraussetzungen für effektives Üben zu schaffen.

Ihr DOWANI Team

Trio Sonata

for two Treble (Alto) Recorders and Basso continuo, TWV 42:F7
F Major / Fa majeur / F-Dur

G. Ph. Telemann (1681 – 1767)
Continuo Realization: M. Zimmermann

DOW 2500

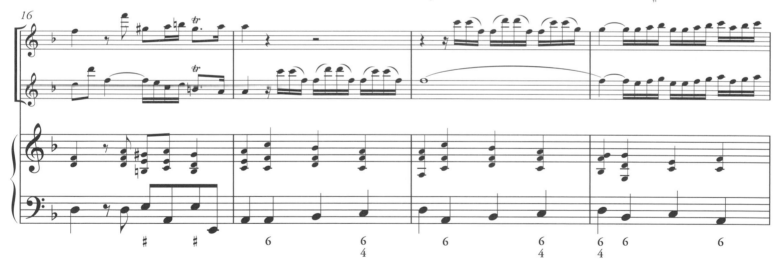

Georg Philipp TELEMANN

(1681 – 1767)

Trio Sonata for 2 Treble (Alto) Recorders
and Basso continuo, TWV 42 : F 7
F Major / Fa majeur / F-Dur

Treble (Alto) Recorder I / Flûte à bec alto I / Altblockflöte I

DOWANI International

Recorder I

Trio Sonata

for two Treble (Alto) Recorders and Basso continuo, TWV 42:F7
F Major / Fa majeur / F-Dur

G. Ph. Telemann (1681 – 1767)

DOW 2500

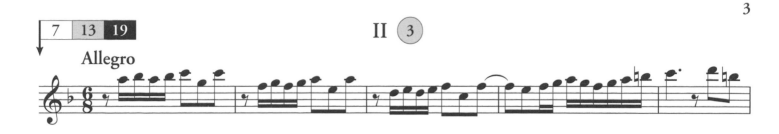

II ③

Allegro

4

III ④

Adagio

IV ⑤

Vivace

piano

forte

Georg Philipp
TELEMANN

(1681 – 1767)

Trio Sonata for 2 Treble (Alto) Recorders
and Basso continuo, TWV 42 : F 7
F Major / Fa majeur / F-Dur

Treble (Alto) Recorder II / Flûte à bec alto II / Altblockflöte II

DOWANI International

Trio Sonata

for two Treble (Alto) Recorders and Basso continuo, TWV 42:F7
F Major / Fa majeur / F-Dur

G. Ph. Telemann (1681 – 1767)

DOW 2500

25 | 31 | 37

Allegro
Rec. I

26 | 32 | 38

4

III   ④

Adagio

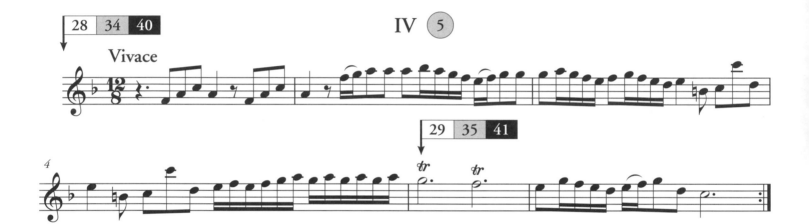

IV   ⑤

Vivace

piano

forte

Georg Philipp TELEMANN

(1681 – 1767)

Trio Sonata for 2 Treble (Alto) Recorders
and Basso continuo, TWV 42 : F 7
F Major / Fa majeur / F-Dur

Basso continuo / Basse continue / Generalbass

DOWANI International

Basso continuo

Trio Sonata

for two Treble (Alto) Recorders and Basso continuo, TWV 42:F7

F Major / Fa majeur / F-Dur

G. Ph. Telemann (1681 – 1767)

I

II

DOW 2500

III

Adagio

IV

Vivace

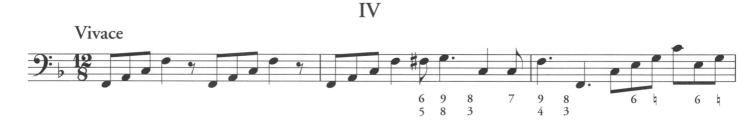

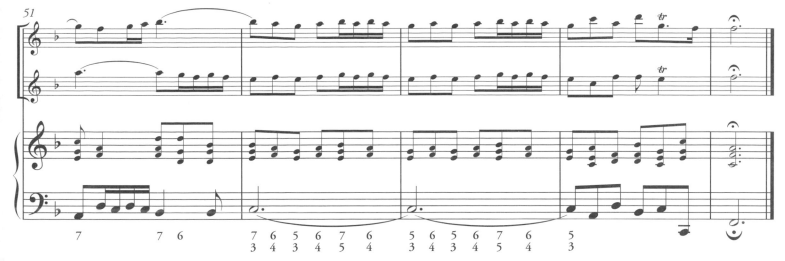

Vivace

Vivace

ENGLISH

DOWANI CD:
- Track No. 1
- Track numbers in circles
- Track numbers in squares

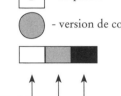

- slow Play Along Tempo
- intermediate Play Along Tempo
- original Play Along Tempo

1	- tuning notes
●	- concert version

- Additional tracks for longer movements or pieces
- **Concert version:** recorder I and II with harpsichord
- **Slow tempo:** harpsichord accompaniment and recorder II with recorder I in the background / harpsichord accompaniment and recorder I with recorder II in the background
- **Intermediate tempo:** harpsichord accompaniment and recorder II / harpsichord accompaniment and recorder I
- **Original tempo:** harpsichord accompaniment and recorder II / harpsichord accompaniment and recorder I

FRANÇAIS

DOWANI CD :
- Plage N° 1
- N° de plage dans un cercle
- N° de plage dans un rectangle

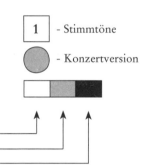

- tempo lent play along
- tempo moyen play along
- tempo original play along

1	- diapason
●	- version de concert

- Plages supplémentaires pour mouvements ou morceaux longs
- **Version de concert :** flûte à bec I et II avec clavecin
- **Tempo lent :** accompagnement de clavecin et flûte à bec II avec flûte à bec I en fond sonore / accompagnement de clavecin et flûte à bec I avec flûte à bec II en fond sonore
- **Tempo moyen :** accompagnement de clavecin et flûte à bec II / accompagnement de clavecin et flûte à bec I
- **Tempo original :** accompagnement de clavecin et flûte à bec II / accompagnement de clavecin et flûte à bec I

DEUTSCH

DOWANI CD:
- Track Nr. 1
- Trackangabe im Kreis
- Trackangabe im Rechteck

- langsames Play Along Tempo
- mittleres Play Along Tempo
- originales Play Along Tempo

1	- Stimmtöne
●	- Konzertversion

- Zusätzliche Tracks bei längeren Sätzen oder Stücken
- **Konzertversion:** Blockflöte I und II mit Cembalo
- **Langsames Tempo:** Cembalobegleitung und Blockflöte II mit Blockflöte I im Hintergrund / Cembalobegleitung und Blockflöte I mit Blockflöte II im Hintergrund
- **Mittleres Tempo:** Cembalobegleitung und Blockflöte II / Cembalobegleitung und Blockflöte I
- **Originaltempo:** Cembalobegleitung und Blockflöte II / Cembalobegleitung und Blockflöte I

DOWANI - 3 Tempi Play Along is published by:
DOWANI International Est.
Industriestrasse 24 / Postfach 156, FL-9487 Bendern,
Principality of Liechtenstein
Phone: ++423 370 11 15, Fax ++423 370 19 44
Email: info@dowani.com
www.dowani.com

Recording & Digital Mastering: M. Schlubeck, Germany & V. Sincek, Croatia
CD-Production: MediaMotion, The Netherlands
Music Notation: Notensatz Thomas Metzinger, Germany
Design: Andreas Haselwanter, Austria
Printed by: Zrinski d.d., Croatia
Made in the Principality of Liechtenstein

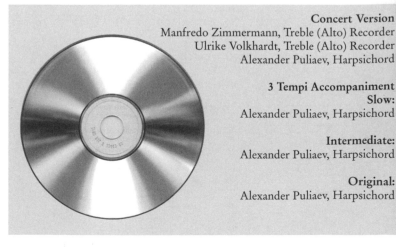

Concert Version
Manfredo Zimmermann, Treble (Alto) Recorder
Ulrike Volkhardt, Treble (Alto) Recorder
Alexander Puliaev, Harpsichord

3 Tempi Accompaniment
Slow:
Alexander Puliaev, Harpsichord

Intermediate:
Alexander Puliaev, Harpsichord

Original:
Alexander Puliaev, Harpsichord